HIGH TOUCH TACTILE DESIGN AND VISUAL EXPLORATIONS

gestalten

CONTENTS

PRE-FACE

Poised between reality and representation, peculiar designery creations continue to flourish beyond page and screen. Spurred by the interdisciplinary mindset of our time, creatives from a variety of fields cut across disciplinary borders to translate their ideas into material objects and spatial orchestrations. The space they enter provides them—as well as us, the jaded spectators of a digitized era—with fresh air to breathe. The power of sensory experience fuels emotions, inspires, and persuades.

Touch is the most private of all senses, unlike sight, which is the one most catered to. Countering image overload and the public availability of almost everything, tangible design enjoys a boom in popularity. Like its precursory volumes, *Tactile* and *Tangible*, *High Touch* observes and documents a movement of inventiveness: the new era of arts and crafts that does not cease to astound and inspire us.

Featured here is the work of a heterogeneous group of creatives working within and across fields: graphic designers, illustrators, and photographers enter the third dimension, team up with or act as craftsmen, architects, and fine artists to play out keen, creative visions. In refusal of the way we categorize and educate creative disciplines as separate drawers of thought, they look into areas as diverse as engineering, set design, and urban planning for material and ideas, dabble at sculpture, product, and landscape design.

The sense of creative inclusiveness muddies territorial waters and broadens minds. Based on the richness of creative disciplines, skillful and oftentimes unusual combinations occur. This selection is diverse, but tied together by the creative acclaim of the high touch.

THE HIGH TOUCH

As a design process, high touch design harnesses psycho-physiological knowledge to develop user-friendly products and humane environments. As one of the most striking aspects of today's visual culture, it suggests a willingness to design experience-centered rather than seamlessly.

While the world moves toward abstraction, perfection, and surface finish, many creatives appear to be stimulated by a certain need for escape. If bygone rebels of design experimentation, like those lumped together under the label of deconstruction, rose up against conventions of form and composition, many contemporary renegades focus on conceptual innovation. Turning from digital abstraction to a relish in experiencing, they resort to tangible particularities and experiment with technique, materiality, scope, and scale. In a world in which efficiency and the speedy transmission of information tends to be considered more important than content, they confront the instability of attention with painstakingly handcrafted compositions that require a certain intensity of awareness. Boiling ambitious ideas down to the material level, they spare no effort. Investing a whole lot of real life time, they charge them with true-to-life-significance.

Genuine manifestations of deep personal involvement, works like Bovey Lee's imply obsession bordering madness. Her incredibly detailed paper-cut illustrations could be produced with ease—industrially, by an automatic or human manufacturing robot. But that would be far off the point: What's crucial and virtually invaluable, about works like Lee's, is the astounding level of humanly commitment captured in the process.

Paper, the graphic designers' and illustrators' home base, is just one among plenty of materials the creatives featured here choose to engage with. Starting with collages, papercraft objects, and multimedia assemblages, their constructs also integrate textiles, food, everyday objects, and heavy-duty material. Absorbed into the formal qualities of materiality and construction, many ideas take more lifelike shape than their makers' theoretically drenched approaches may suggest.

Filippo Minelli and Ujin Lee, for example, deliberately choose to work in non-permanent mediums and probe the world's immaterial fabric with spellbinding, ephemeral scenes of dust and smoke. Works like these remain aloof—untouchable products of momentary sensual perception. Processes are factored in: chemical reactions, fermentations, color changes, decay, and desiccation become integral parts of the creative concept. Side by side with experiments of scientific ambition stand playful explorations, works that appear to be based on fortunate aesthetic happenstance. More often than not, what counts is not pictures, but events.

REALITY AND REPRESENTATION

ART AND TECHNOLOGY

It is in the face of digital abstraction that the estimation of the real rises. Key is the unique presence in time and space—what Walter Benjamin in his seminal essay "The Work of Art in the Age of Mechanical Reproduction," defines as Aura. The spacio-temporal structure itself becomes the medium, offering a concrete, one-off experience directly to the addressee. Opposed to the auratic value of the original work are the compositional features of its reproduced instance.

Some of the projects compiled in this volume are conceived primarily to be seen in reproduction. In these cases, the tangible composition represents an interim stage, something to be reproduced in flat media at some point. Such works may lose their literal tangibility and the Aura of the original, but gain an additional contextual layer through the process of reproduction itself. Meaning, here, lies in the composition, and in the expressively loaded tension between original and reproduction. What's authentic is the act of realization, what's real is the setting of the scene.

The sense of the real changes with tradition. Neither matter nor space nor time has been what it was since Walter Benjamin defined the phenomena of Aura in the thirties. Reproduction has gone digital, accelerated significantly as to both pace and edition. Mass reproduction and the immediate availability of almost everything are key principles of our time that continue to change modes and habits of human sense perception. Ever-present throughout this selection of works is the quarrel with the relation between original and reproduction, and the perpetual probing of our notion of authenticity.

Bravely reorganizing the "how-does-representation-relate-to-the-real" hypothetical, the creatives featured here take free reign to tell genuine, visual stories that are thoughtful but not ponderous; pointed but not didactic. It is surprising how their lifelike qualities subsist in reproduction. Occasionally, the photograph appropriates the actual, physical instance.

Staged to enter the two-dimensional realm of print media, works like Katrin Schacke's draw us into dynamic scenes of action. Turning readers into spectators and format restrictions into creative opportunity, they present themselves as vivid reminders of Marshall McLuhan's famous claim for media validity: "Today we are beginning to notice that the new media are not just mechanical gimmicks for creating worlds of illusion, but new languages with new and unique powers of expression."

As always, the state of the art takes full effect on the state of the arts. Technological developments incite creative action. The digital shift changes paradigms of thought and design production. As a democratizing and connecting force, the web allows for peer-to-peer interdisciplinary networking, open source working processes, self-publishing, self-organized learning, and knowledge sharing. Global connectivity inspires and facilitates radical form.

While countering the internet's infinite, fleeting stream of content with time-consumingly crafted, intricate, and hand-made creations, many of the works in this book are closely allied with technology, digital production, and reproduction, and most are realized with the aid of—or at least refined by—computers and technological tools. Although it is due to the possibilities of technical manipulation that particular idiosyncratic visions find a way to come alive, the issue is marked by controversy. There is high tech with high touch, high touch quality vs. high tech gadgetry, or the commitment to both.

TOYING WITH TRUTH

Many times, the pragmatics of technological circumstances are covered by the transcendental daze of surrealism. Some creations appear magical to the point of being absurd and confusing and seem to lack—or rather attack—meaning. Others propose a pure, somewhat mind-boggling understanding of things, and raise it for a while above the constitutive narrowness of common sense. Dorota Buczkowska's levitating swing, for example, tricks the laws of nature for the benefit of a truly dreamlike sight to behold. Ordinary life and its rules and regulations are temporarily suspended, reversed, or responded to with startling creative wit.

Dispensing with Cagean reminiscence, some makers blazingly challenge the role of creative composition and its relation to reality. Not only do they implement utterly unconventional, often visceral and evocative, materials, they also apply them in ways antithetical to the subject itself. Celebrating the power of transmutation and the mythical singularity of the condition, they bring forth paradoxisms and baroque confusion. With humor and the grotesque they wed the sacred with the profane.

Any conceptual approach involves the effort to liberate imagination. Embracing reality to play with the loss of it, some works present themselves as visual science fiction; their art lies in their invention. Allowing for associations that tend to be neglected by reason, they promote idiosyncrasies, creative alternatives and the desire to change the world—or at least to look at it with fresh eyes.

Surreal compositions and erratic arrangements demand constant scrutiny; the unexpected and seemingly improper configuration of the subject and its material representation questions the notion of objective identity. Truth is endlessly tested and contested—and challenged by a new phenomenology of composition, in which elements are juxtaposed and held together by sole virtue of their wondrous liaison.

SPIRITUAL ROOTS

Experimenting with material, scale, and scope, and space works like Nils Nova's, Frank Kunert's or Ron van der Ende's create friction, call forth multiple associations and encourage the viewer to contemplate. It is due to intriguing contextual composition that we respond with awe and wonder. Unusual settings and abstruse setups bring forth a sense of strangeness and irritation that relates back to sixties anti-art and its original premise of subversion.

In fact, the selection here is drenched with compelling citations and ascendancies of bygone artistic movements. There are works bearing resemblance to Picasso's *Still Life with Chair Caning*, which is often referred to as the first assemblage. Others appear to follow the vain of Duchamp, the originator of the ready-mades, who famously blurred the borders between life and art. If Liesbet Buusche's urban jewellery or Rómulo Celdráns oversized objects echo Pop Art, it is the precise geometry of Russian Costructivism that resonates in the peculiar creations of Kulte. Frédérique Daubal's works *Big Eyes* and *Big Mouth* resound with a certain Dadaist irrationality, Lucas Simões collaged portraits resemble Op Art in structure, and Alt Group's *Silo Theatre* possesses the same sense of subconscious fluidity as many surrealist paintings.

A certain postmodernist conceptualism seems inherent to most of them: whether you repeat a Campbell soup can 50 times on a canvas, knit a hot dog, set up three-dimensional stills from *The Simpsons*, or zoom in on germs to render them in glass—the focus is shifted from the retinal image of the object itself to the otherwise incomprehensible idea that makes you want to portray it that way. As Allan Kaprow noted in his essays on the blurring of art and life, "it is not life in general that is meaningful; an abstraction can't be experienced. Only life in particular can be—some tangible aspect of it serving as a representative, for example, a ripe summer tomato."

RAISON D'ETRE AND REAL WORLD REFERENCE

Referring to so-called fine art precedence is not to fall short of the large number of commissioned, designery projects that are part of this selection. In their attempt to achieve a sense of contemplation in the minds of their intended audience, some, like Byggstudio's sign concept for Folkets Park, stay relatively close to design's purposive sphere of action. Presented side by side with self-initiated, theoretically drenched endeavors that break rather radically with design's utilitarian application, they, too, induce an experience-based state of integrity.

Inviting the spectator out into a transitional space that weaves back and forth across the borders between the conceptual and the commercial—this is also the space they themselves inhabit as makers, as they move between audiences, clients, creative modes, and creative ideologies, from the occasional experience of disciplinary exile to cherished idiosyncrasy.

Some of the featured creatives wield a range of graphic design essentials—like spacing, typography, color, or arrangement—but they wield them like newfangled weapons, seizing the ammunition of everyday life. With works that are safely anchored in the concrete realities of our familiar surroundings and its everyday objects and conditions, they emphasize the inextricability of design and life. Every day, occasion, and environment may serve as setting, technical framework, as a theme, or inspiration.

SNEAK PREVIEW

As diverse as their worldly, inspirational source pool, the works at hand speak a variety of different dialects. Austere and unique in style, with their peculiar material and structure, they indicate a shift of syntax and vocabulary in the language of design. Ranging from plain modernism to baroque grandeur, they defy any attempt of clear-cut categorization. Roughly broken down into eight sections, the selection highlights a range of significant thematic clusters.

Mirror Mirror, for instance, exemplifies that the notion of high touch bears close relation to that of the humane. Featuring a range of peculiar experiments in fashion and fabric, body and medium, it illustrates that the notion of identity is an alienating concept for the individual to intellectually consider. Undermined by social structure and concepts like religion and ideology, the self has always been a key subject of creative inquiry. Nowadays, the domain of cyberspace breeds online identities and digital profiles that call for a palpable opposition. Seriously dedicated to garments and their engineering, some creatives, such as Daisy Balloon, construct true architectures of dress. Others, like Femke Agema, introduce carnivalesque weirdness to editorial fashion spreads, and Robert Hardgrave brings alienating costumes to art gallery settings. Poised between authenticity and eccentricity, the natural joy of dressing up and masquerading is turned into creative "truth games" that add new perspectives to human self-conception and contemporary creative practice.

If artists like Picasso first famously introduced everyday things to the canvas to free the painting from the constraints of two-dimensionality, it is the contemporary creatives pooled in the aptly titled section **Space Invaders** who spin the thought out. Gregory Euclide, for example, does so quite literally: eliciting the artwork from its flatness, he allows it to brim over its frame. Michael Johansson works at the threshold between painterly tradition and spatiality, too, but reverses the approach: assigned to an earlier chapter called **Director's Cut**, his arrangement of household objects covers the full wall of a room, and thus appears plane, like a still life, or a quasi-plane collage.

Space is entered throughout the book, but addressed in particular over the course of the final chapters: here, dimensions expand somewhat gradually, from delicately layered collage work, to wall reliefs, mural-like backdrops, and miniature sceneries, all the way to expansive walk-in installations and environments.

Gathered under the title **Gulliver's Travels** are examples concerned with the issue of scale and proportion. We encounter Isaac Cordal's miniature characters that confront the world's unseizable vastness with the meticulous touch of model makers, and Frank Kunert's sceneries that imitate the real with painstaking exactitude. The chapter **Trompe L'œil** focuses on optical illusions, and features works as intriguing as Nils Nova's particularly site-specific photo installations, which make use of an old set design trick to deceive our assumptions about space and perspective.

The list could go on, but trusting that pictures are worth more than lengthy descriptions, we prefer to just draw the curtain for this fine selection of high touch projects and creative explorations. They begin with the possibilities of tangible material, proceed with the unlikeliness of its application, and present visual culture as an organic, evolutionary process that is never fixed and finished.

GULLIVER'S TRAVELS

"Anyone who doesn't take truth seriously in small matters cannot be trusted in large ones either."

Albert Einstein

Sørensen–Grundy
1   Construction Overhead
2012, buckram, wire, 100 % worsted wool, Model: Abigail Bates, Photo: Simon Monk

Isaac Cordal
2   CCTV Parasite
3   Aborigen
4   Remembrances from Nature
2009–2011
Photos: Isaac Cordal

Isaac Cordal
[1] Playground
[2] Follow the Leaders
2010
Photos: Isaac Cordal

Christopher Boffoli
3 Barricade Challenger
4 Strawberry Seed Harvesters
5 Cupcake Golfer
2009–2011
Photos: Christopher Boffoli

Liliana Porter
Man with Axe
Hosfelt Gallery, New York, 2011,
Photo: David Stroud

Tessa Farmer
Little Savages
The Natural History Museum,
London, 2007, taxidermied
fox and bird, wasp nest, dried
toads, animal bones, insects,
plant roots, Courtesy The Natural History Museum London
and Danielle Arnaud, London,
Photos: Christopher Boffoli &
Tessa Farmer

Gregory Euclide

Frank Kunert
1 Sunny Side
  2004, foamcore, cardboard,
  wood, doll equipment, fabric,
  dried plants, flints
2 Tennis Half-Pipe
  2002, foamcore, cardboard,
  miniature trees
3 Upstairs Toilets
  2010, foamcore, cardboard,
  wire, acrylic glass
Photos: Frank Kunert

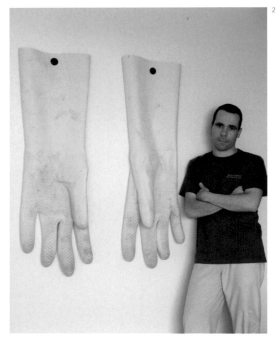

Rómulo Celdrán
1   Macro IX
     2012, polychromed aluminum,
     synthetic material, epoxi resin
2   Macro I
     2008, polychromed polystyrene
3   Macro V
     2009, polychromed polystyrene
4   Reality Bites I
     2010, polychromed polystyrene
     Photos: Rómulo Celdrán

Christopher Jarratt
5   Hairbrush
     2005, English cherry, refinished
     reclaimed golf balls
6   Slingshots—Vermillion
     2011, timber: English sycamore
     (giant slingshot), English beech
     (small slingshots), silicon rub-
     ber, Italian leather

Liesbet Bussche
1   Urban Jewelry
    Fubon Art Foundation, Taiwan,
    2011, plastic globes, light bulbs,
    electrical wire
2-4 Urban Jewelry
    2009, brass, wood, paint, steel

Florentijn Hofman

1 **Fat Monkey**
Pixel Show, São Paulo, 2010,
inflatable, rope, flip flops,
Photo: Raquel Brust

2 **Stor Gul Kanin
(Big Yellow Rabbit)**
OpenArt Biennale Örebro, 2011,
wood, shingles, metal, concrete,
Photo: Courtesy of Florentijn
Hofman

next spread **Steelman**
Client: Municipality of Amster-
dam Slotervaart, 2011,
concrete, paint, anti-graffiti
coating, Photo: Frank Hanswijk

Ron van der Ende

1. Corsair
2. s.t. (Wood Stack)
3. Still Life
   2010–2011, bas-relief in
   salvaged wood

TROMPE L'ŒIL

—————

"Everything we see hides another thing, we always want to see what is hidden by what we see."

Magritte

Ron van der Ende
1 Mum (Grand Pianola Piece)
2 Breaker
3 Silver Machine (Lotus Turbo Esprit 1983)
2007–2011, bas-relief in salvaged wood

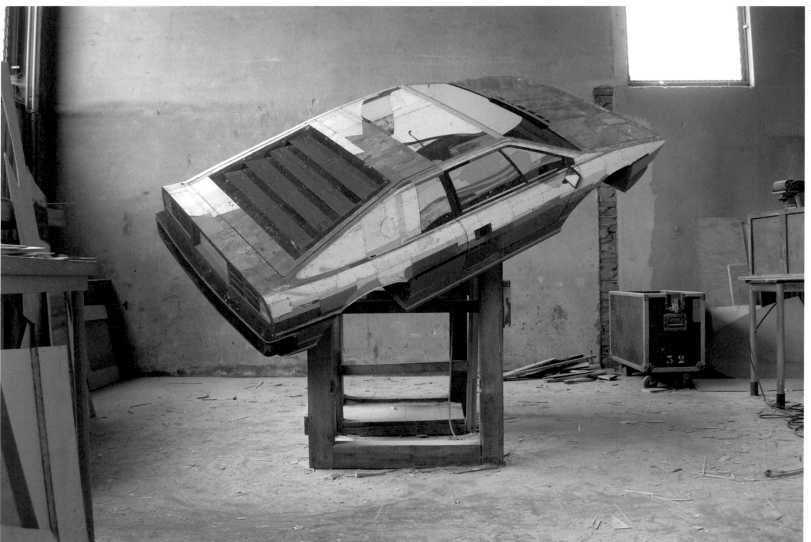

4

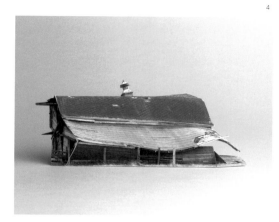

5

6

James Hopkins
1 Tom & Jerry
   2005, acrylic plastic,
   Private collection
2 Family Portrait
   2006, acrylic plastic
   Courtesy of the artist and
   Jacob's Island Gallery
3 Kyle, Stan, Cartman & Kenny
   2006, acrylic plastic,
   Private collection
4 Role Reversal
   2005, acrylic plastic,
   Courtesy of the artist and
   Jacob's Island Gallery

Michael Murphy
1 Katie (expanded graphic)
   2011, acrylic,
   Photo: Michael Murphy

James Hopkins
2 Beauty Spot
   2007, bronze and wood base,
   Courtesy of the artist and
   Jacob's Island Gallery
3 Impossible World
   2002, wooden stool,
   Courtesy of the artist and
   Jacob's Island Gallery

John V. Muntean
4 Cow Cow Cow
   2010, mahogany with wax
   finish, stainless steel, acrylic
5-6 Dancers
   2012, mahogany with wax
   finish, stainless steel, acrylic
   Photos: J. V. Muntean

3

4

5

6

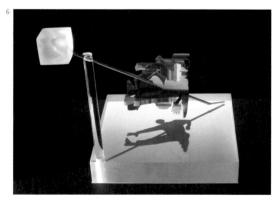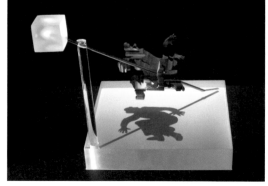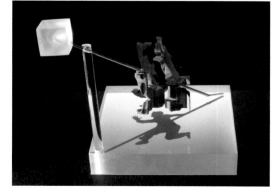

Nils Nova
[1] Im Gegenlicht
Hilfikerfoto Luzern, 2009
[2-3] **Mind the Gap**
Kunsthaus Glarus, 2008,
Inkjet on paper
Photos: Nils Nova

Leandro Erlich

1–3 **Bâtiment**
Nuit Blanche, Paris, 2004, metal
frame, print, mirror, lights,
Photos: Leandro Erlich Studio
& Henriette Desjonquères and
Paul Fargues

4–5 **Tsumari House**
Echigo Tsumari Art Triennale,
Japan, 2006, metal frame, print,
mirror, lights, Photos: Leandro
Erlich Studio

Zander Olsen
1–5 Tree, Line
     2004–2010
1   Untitled (Cader)
2   Beeches
3   Jhutti
4   Duncan Wood
5   Cadair, Oak

41

Jasmin Schuller

1–3 Sweet Meat
2011, blood, lard, meat, Digital
Art Direction: Aleksandar Sto-
janovic, Assistant: Katharina
Oberegger

IMITATION OF LIFE

———

"Don't we all just really try to fake it well?"

Yancy Butler

Chen Chen

1 Cold Cuts Coasters
   2011, wood, fabric, resin, epoxy
   clay, various other materials,
   Collaborative project with
   Kai Williams

Ed Bing Lee

2 Cupcake with Sprinkles
   2006, waxed linen, cotton

3 Burger II
   Private collection, 2006,
   waxed linen, linen, cotton,
   synthetic ribbons

4 Pumpkin Pie
   2006, waxed linen, raffia
   Photos: Ken Yanoviak

Henry Hargreaves

5 Food of the Rainbow
   2010, Photo: Henry Hargreaves,
   Styling: Lisa Edslav

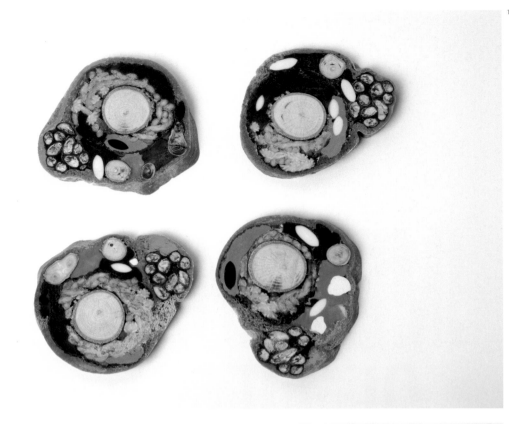

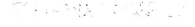

44

45

Kyle Bean
1–4 **Soft Weapons**
    Client: CUT Magazine, 2011,
    Photos: Sam Hofman
1   **Ice Cream Dynamite**
    ice cream lollies, wire, timer
2   **Feather Knife**
    feather, plastic handle
3   **Jelly Grenade**
    jelly, paper plate
4   **Bread Knuckle Dusters**
    bread, wooden board, knife

Kyle Bean
What Came First?
2011, eggshells, papier-mâché

Kyle Bean
1-2 Stick Insects
     2010, matchsticks,
     Photos: Owen Silverwood
1   Beetle
2   Dragonfly

Sayaka Ganz

1 **Emergence**
2008, reclaimed plastic objects, painted metal, wire

2 **Night**
2008, reclaimed black and clear plastic objects, wire

Anna-Wili Highfield

3 **Wolf**
2012, ink, watercolor paint, archival cotton paper, cotton thread, wooden base

4 **Seahorse**
2011, ink, watercolor paint, archival cotton paper, copper rod, timber block

5 **Australian Magpie**
2010, ink, shellac, archival cotton paper, cotton thread, brass rod, timber block

6 **Panda**
Client: WWF, 2011, ink, watercolor paint, archival cotton paper, cotton thread, wooden base

7 **White Bellied Sea Eagle**
2010, ink, watercolor paint, archival cotton paper, cotton thread, copper pipe, timber block

8 **Black Fronted Dotterel**
2010, ink, watercolor, archival cotton paper, cotton thread, brass rod, timber block

Laurel Roth

1   Beauty
     2011, mixed media including
     fake fingernails, nail polish, bar-
     rettes, false eyelashes, jewelry,
     walnut, Swarovski crystals

2   Beloved
     2007, fake fingernails, false
     eyelashes, barrettes, dimestore
     jewelry, wood, pewter, Swarovski
     crystals, nail polish

3   Plumage
     2010, mixed media including
     fake fingernails, nail polish, bar-
     rettes, false eyelashes, jewelry,
     walnut, Swarovski crystals

4   Regalia
     2011, mixed media including
     fake fingernails, nail polish, bar-
     rettes, false eyelashes, jewelry,
     walnut, Swarovski crystals
     Photos: Andy Diaz Hope

The Makerie Studio

5   The Great Omar
     Client: Sangorski & Sutcliffe,
     2010, hand-printed oriental
     paper, glue, Swarovski crystals

6-7 The White Omar
     2011, iridescent paper, glue,
     Swarovski crystals, Photos:
     Nathan Gallagher

Shawn Smith

1 **Arctic Game**
2006, MDF, acrylic paint,
Photo: Teresa Rafidi

2 **8bit Campfire**
2005, 1 cm plastic cubes, spray paint

3 **Peafile**
2006, plywood, ink, acrylic paint

4 **Mahi Mahi**
2006, plywood, ink, acrylic paint ,
Photo: Teresa Rafidi

5 **Vaquity**
2007, plywood, ink, acrylic paint,
Photo: Ann Berman

6 **Double Dahl**
2007, plywood, ink, acrylic paint ,
Photo: Teresa Rafidi

7 **Game**
2006, plywood, Photo: Ann Berman

8 **Kept**
2009, bass wood, ink, acrylic paint,
found bird cage , Photo: Teresa Rafidi

Clémentine Henrion
1 Helium Eternal
   2009, balloons made of metallic
   fabric, duchess satin, polyester
   fibers, Photos: Joan Braun

Kiel Johnson
2 SLR #1
3 Polaroid #2
4 SLR #3
5 SLR #5
6 SLR #7
7 Twin Lens #2
   2010, chipboard, tape,
   acrylic sealer
   Photos: Theo Jemison

Kiel Johnson

8 The Observatory
2011, plywood, pine, chipboard, conduit, acrylic, Photos: Will Tee Yang & Kiel Johnson

Jennifer Collier

9   Paper Singer Sewing Machine
10 Paper Telephone
11 Paper Typewriter
2011, Found Paper and Stitch
Photos: Gareth Perry

Jonathan Brand

1 **One Piece at a Time**
Hosfelt Gallery New York, 2011,
cut and folded archival inkjet
prints on paper, PVA glue,
foamboard, Photo: Laura
Desantis-Olsson

2 **Fallen**
2007, carved MDF, wood glue,
hardwood dowels

3 **Motor**
2011, cut and folded archival
inkjet prints on paper, PVA glue

3

Don Lucho / Luis Valdés
 Car-Toon Crash
 2009, wood structure, cardboard, paper, masking tape,
 paint, Photo: Martin La Roche

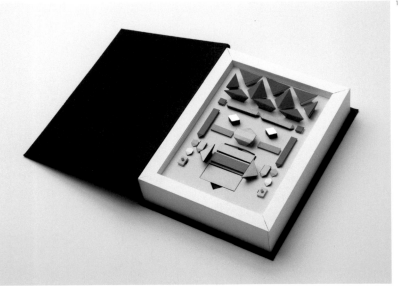

66

PAPER TIGER

"Paint with whatever material you please—with pipes, postage stamps, postcards or playing cards, painted paper, or newspapers."

Guillaume Apollinaire

Eva Jauss
1   Facebook
     2009, paper
2   Urbanity
     2009, paper (letterpress embossed)
     Photos: Michael Breyer

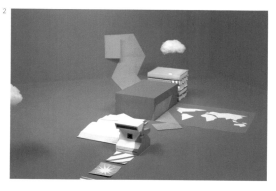

Lobulo Design
1   Cover, H Magazine
    2010, different kinds of paper,
    Photo: Lobulo Design

Greg Barth
2–6 7TV Rebranding
2   Travel Ident
3   Cinema Ident
4   Changing Yourself Ident
5   Relationships Ident
6   Construction Ident
     Client: 7TV RUSSIA, 2011,
     wood, paper, cardboard, cotton
     Music and Sound Design: Noo-
     kaad Productions, Project Man-
     ager: Colas Wohlfahrt, Producer
     and D.O.P: Noe Sardet, Lead
     Builders: Ian Langhor & Clem-
     ent Yeh, Set Director: Sylvain
     Lavoie, Builders: Julie Ledru,
     Guillaume Kukucka, Florian
     Golay, Charlotte B. Pelletie

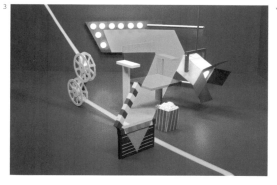

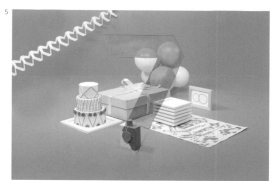

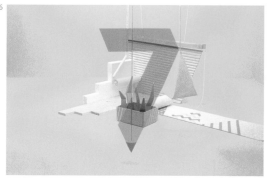

Owen Gildersleeve
1   Quest for Dairy Without the Ouch
Client: Lactofree, 2011, paper diagram with real food and tableware, Photo: Sara Morris
Food Stylist: John Bentham

Lobulo Design
2   Casio G-Shock GA-110
2011
3   Hospital
Client: O, The Oprah Magazine, 2011
Photos: Lobulo Design

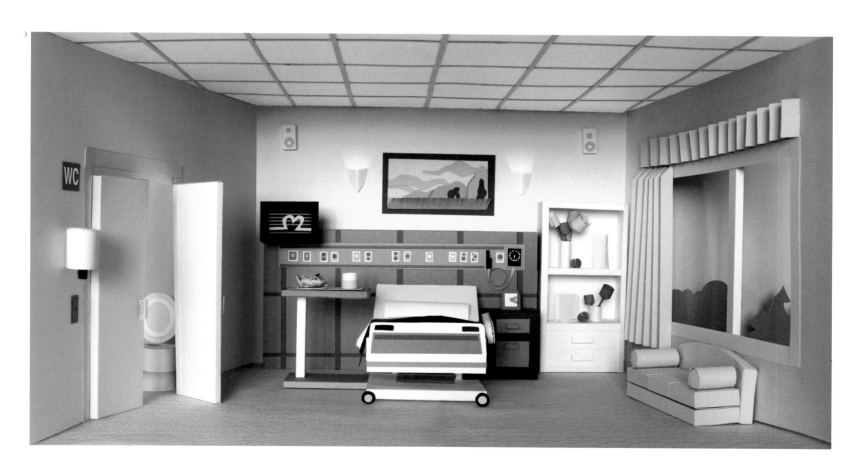

Mandy Smith
 Gramophone
 2012, paper, glue, foamboard,
 Photo: Leon Hendrickx

3

Sarah Applebaum
1 Paper and Wood Head
2012, paper, wood
2 Studio with Picket Signs
2012, wood, paint

Johnny Kelly
3 Don't Panic
Client: Don't Panic, 2009
paper, glue, Design/Model
Build: Johnny Kelly, Photos:
Linda Brownlee
4 Pirate
2008, paper, glue

Armin B. Wagner
& Liddy Scheffknecht
Pop Up
2009, cardboard, tape

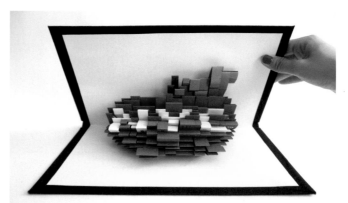

78

Daisy Lew
1–2 Pop-up NYC
     2010, paper

Hvass & Hannibal
3   Ghost of a Chance - Making of
4   Ghost of a Chance
    Client: Turboweekend, 2009,
    folded printed paper,
    Photo: Brian Buchard

Owen Gildersleeve

1 **Video Game Piracy**
   Client: Wired Magazine, 2010,
   paper
2 **Cutting Taxes**
   Client: Money Magazine, 2010,
   paper and US tax forms

Bianca Chang

3 **Dot**
   2011, paper
4 **Twin**
   2011, paper

3
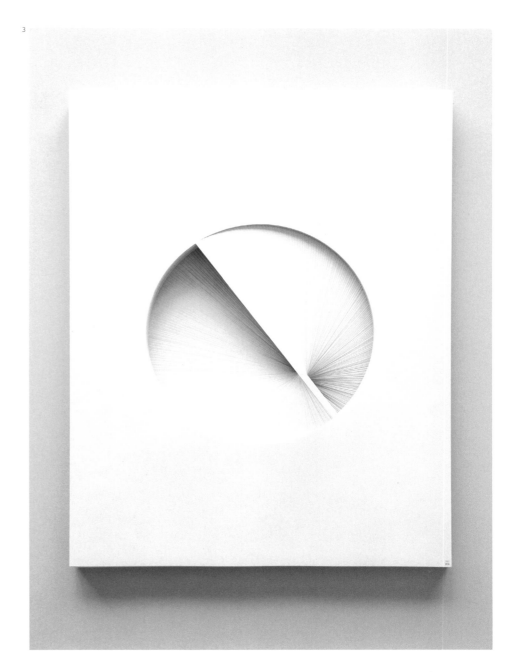

4

Elisabeth Lecourt

1   Réglisse Menthe
    et Barbe Rousse
    2012, map of Italy

2   Baltazar et Anecdote
    2011, map of New York City
    with watercolor

3   Bave de Crapaud
    et Baguette Magique
    2012, map of Niagara Falls

4   Le Petit Canard
    Danseuse Ballerine
    2011, balloon map of London
    rep.1851

5   La Déléguée de Classe
    2012, map of the United States
    of America, gold leaf

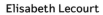

Alida Rosie Sayer

1 Here we are (I.)
2010, hand-cut screen prints
on cartridge paper

2 What I saw (I.)
2011, hand-cut digital prints
on coated paper
Photos: Philip Sayer

Karim Charlebois-Zariffa

3 Moment Factory logo
Client: Moment Factory, 2011
wood, mirrors, wood stain,
Photos: Simon Duhamel

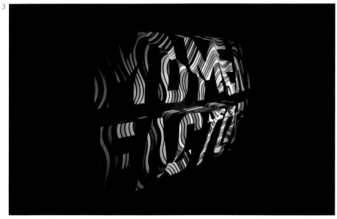

Lauren Clay

4   Emptying Marco Polo's Knapsack
2008, acrylic on cut paper,
acetate

5   Inverted Continuum
2008, acrylic on cut paper,
acrylic mirror, papier-mâché,
wood

6   The Unending Amends We've
Made (Imperishable Wreath)
2010, acrylic on cut paper,
papier-mâché, wire, wood
Photos: Photo 315, Courtesy of
Larissa Goldston Gallery

Nick Georgiou

¹ Vivleia
  2011, discarded books,
  fiberglass, wire, foam
² Tracks
  2011, Tucson Weekly Newspaper, wire, foam
³ The Scholar
  2011, mixed media (discarded
  books, ink) on canvas
  Photos: Nick Georgiou

86

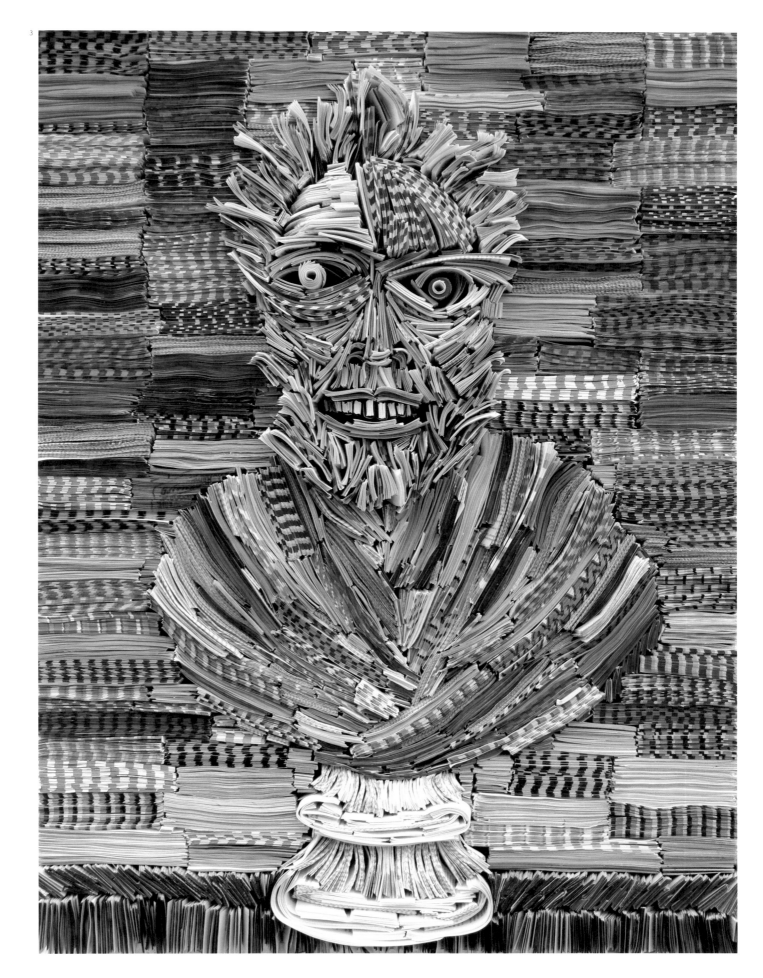

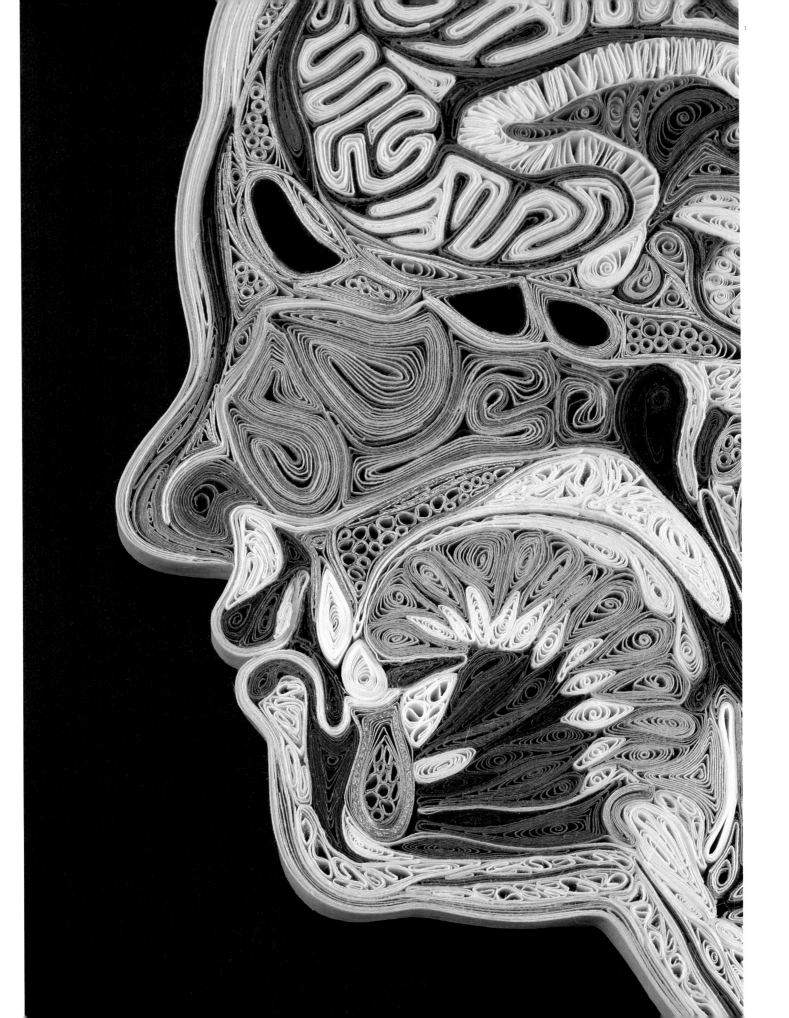

2

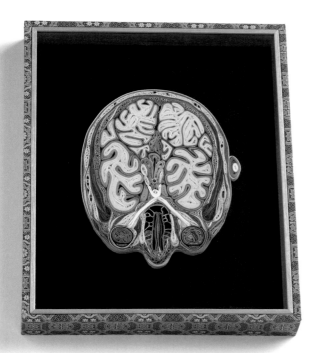

3

Lisa Nilsson
1   Sagittal Section: Head and Torso (detail)
    2010, paper
2   Head I
    2011, paper
3   Head II
    2011, paper
4   Female Torso
    2010, paper
5   Sagittal Section: Head and Torso
    2010, paper
    Photos: John Polak

4

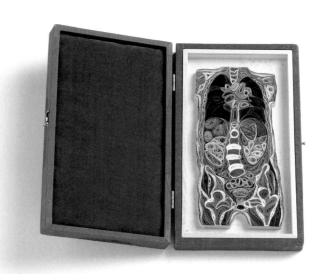

5

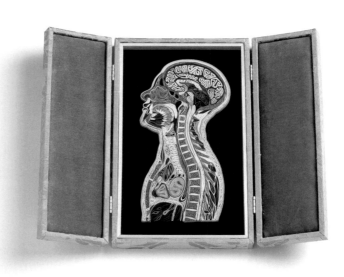

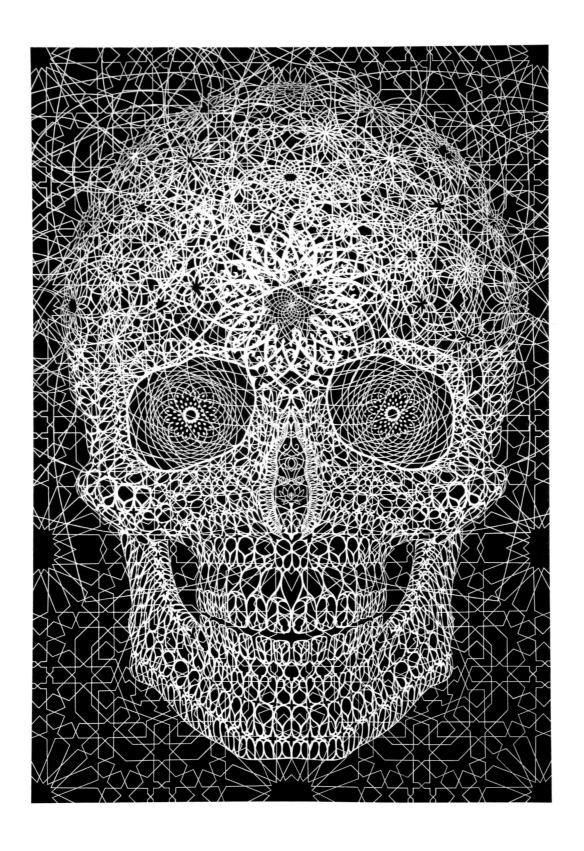

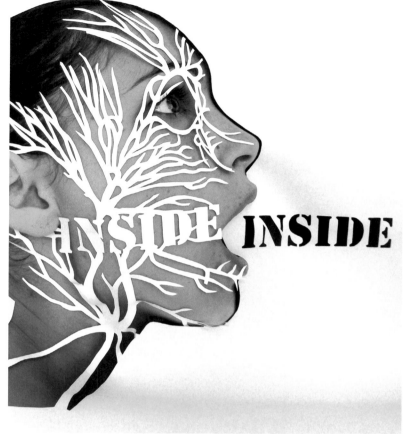

INSIDE

YOUR SKIN

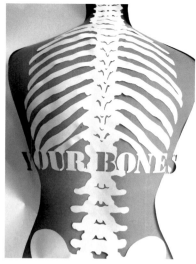

YOUR BONES

IT IS HOW CLOSE IT SITS TO

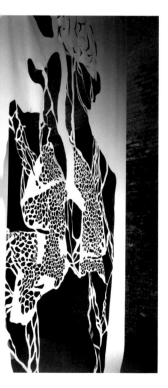

3

Hunter Stabler
1   Hare Christmas Maharishi
    2008, ink and graphite on paper

**Floortje Bouwkamp
in collaboration with Nine Fluitsma**
2   Papercuts
    GreyTones exhibition & book /
    Dutch Design Week, 2006
    paper, poem by Cralan Kelder

Lightning & Kinglyface
3   Cranial Nerve
    Client: Nomad, 2012, paper,
    Photos: Alexandre Guirkinger

Bovey Lee
1–4 **Power Plant**
2008, hand-cut Chinese
rice paper
1 & 4 **The Sacrifice of Dawn**
2–3 **The Butterfly Dream**
Photos: Eddie Lam

STRING THEORY

"What appears to be empty space is actually a tumultuous ocean of strings vibrating at the precise frequencies that create the four dimensions you and I call height, width, depth, and time."

Roy H. Williams

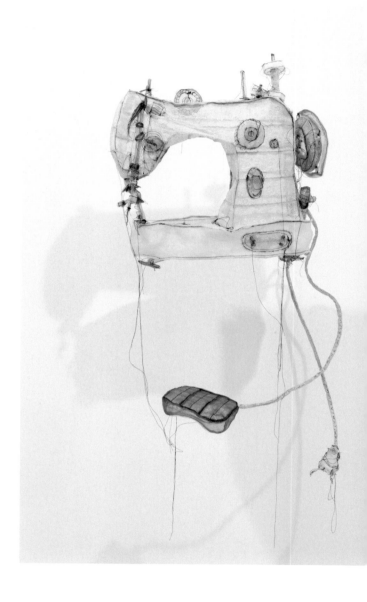

Jannick Deslauriers
1   Poppy Field (detail)
    2009, silk, organza, tulle, thread,
    Photo: Robert Skinner
2   Sewing Machine
    2011, crinoline, organza, lace,
    thread, Photo: Olivier Bousquet

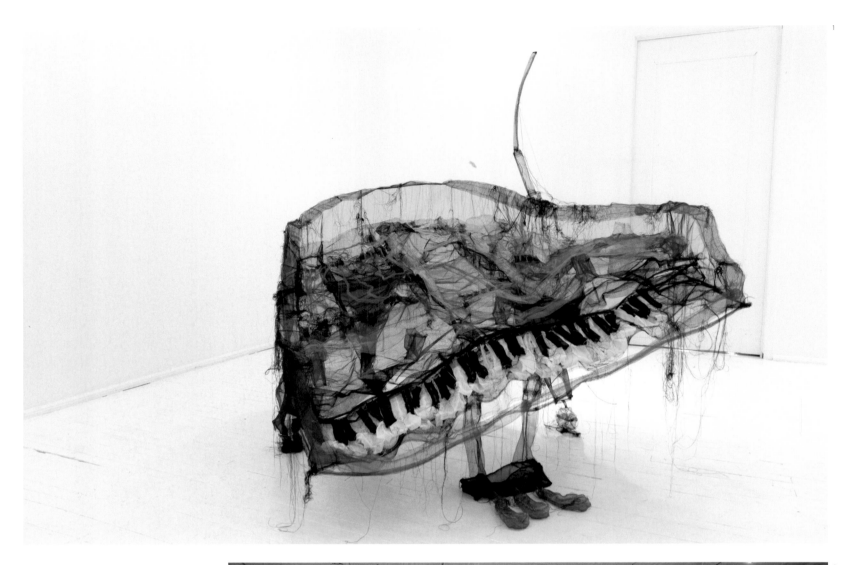

Jannick Deslauriers

1   Piano
   2011, crinoline, tulle, thread,
   Photo: Olivier Bousquet
2   What's Left?
   2010, crinoline, thread,
   Photo: Simon Cole
3   Typewriter
   2011, crinoline, organza, lace,
   thread, Photo: Olivier Bousquet

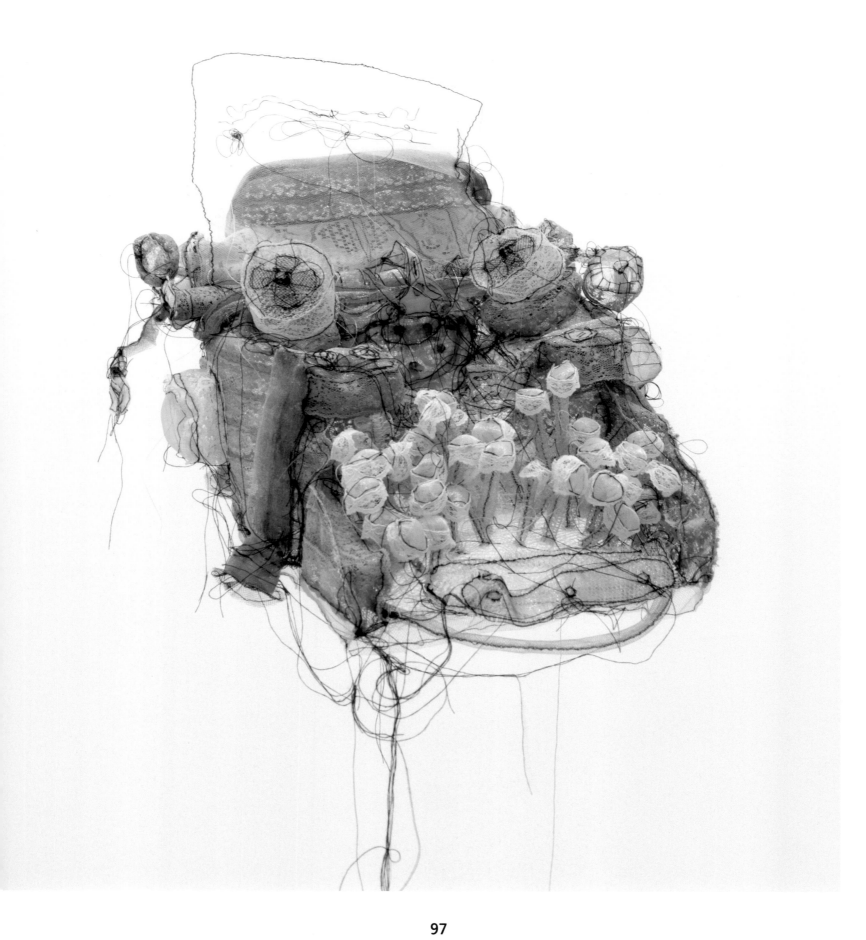

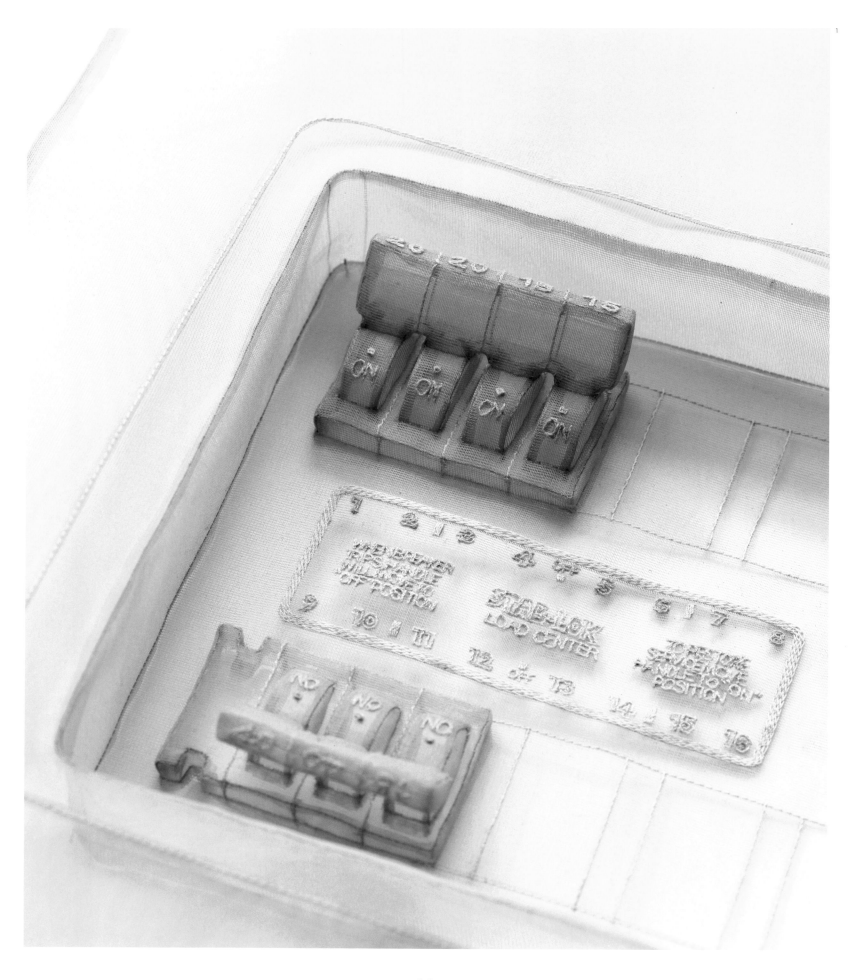

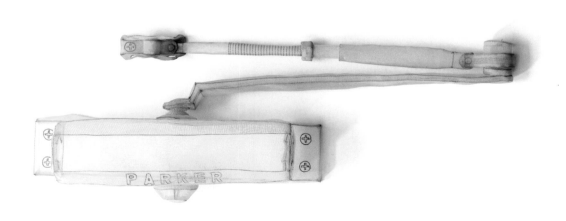

Do Ho Suh

1. Breaker Box, Living Area—Apt. A, 348 West 22nd Street, New York, NY 10011, U.S.A. (detail) 2011, polyester fabric
2. Shower Head, Bathroom—Apt. A, 348 West 22nd Street, New York, NY 10011, U.S.A. 2011, polyester fabric
3. Doorknob + Lock, Entrance—First Floor, 348 West 22nd Street, New York, NY 10011, U.S.A. 2011, polyester fabric
4. Door Closer, Corridor—Ground Floor, 348 West 22nd Street, New York, NY 10011, U.S.A. 2011, polyester fabric, Courtesy of the artist and Lehmann Maupin Gallery, New York

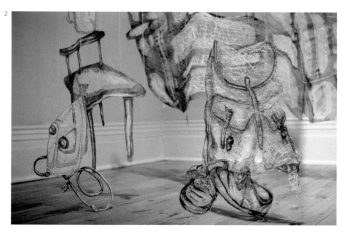

Amanda McCavour
1–2 **Living Room**
2010–2011, thread,
This project was produced
with the support of the
Ontario Arts Council.
Photos: Agata Piskunowicz
3 **Stand-In For Home**
2009–2010, thread,
This project was produced
with the support of the City of
Toronto through the Toronto
Arts Council.

Olek

1 **Knitting is for Pus*****
2010, mixed media,
Olek's crocheted apartment

2 **Crocheted Footbridge**
2005, crocheted acrylic yarn on
a bridge in Poland

3 **Crocheted Cube**
2011, crocheted acrylic yarn on
Astor Place Cube

4 **Crocheted Windows No. 1**
2005, crocheted acrylic yarn

5 **Project b (Wall Street Bull)**
2010, crocheted acrylic yarn on
Wall Street Bull, guerilla action
Photos: Olek

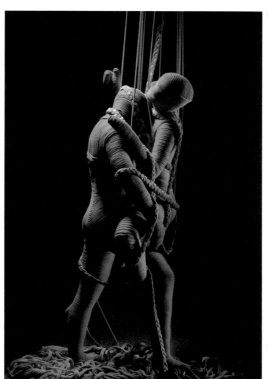

Erik Ravelo
1–4 & next spread Lana Sutra
Client: Benetton, 2011,
plaster, wool, Photos: Courtesy
of Fabrica

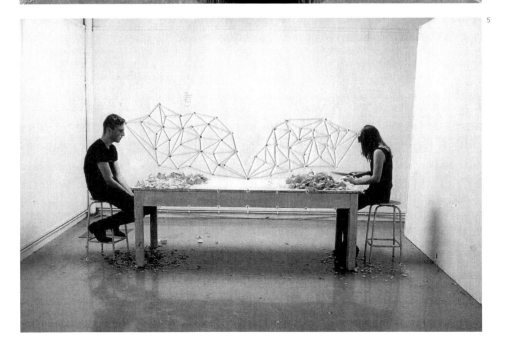

María Aparicio Puentes
1 359
   Galería Maxó, 2011, photo-
   graphic paper (semi-matte
   finish), thread, Photo: Claudio A.
   Troncoso Rojas
2 360
   The Youth Quake, 2011,
   paper print, thread, Photo:
   Claudio A. Troncoso Rojas
3 346
   2011, paper print, thread,
   Photo: Aleksandra Urbanowicz
4 337
   2011, paper print, thread,
   Photo: Dasha Riabchenko
5 363
   2011, paper print, thread,
   Photo: Robbert Geens
6 358
   2011, paper print, thread,
   Photo: Rachel Louise Hodgson

Debbie Smyth

1 Threadbare
Manchester Craft and Design
Centre, 2010, pins, thread

2 Trolleyed
2010, pins, thread

3 Jubilee Bridge
Brindley Arts Centre, Runcorn,
2009, pins, thread
Photos: Zac Mead

L-able

4 NETwork 01
2011, nails, thread on wooden
board, realized by Pamela
Campagna in collaboration with
Thomas Scheiderbauer

5 NETwork 06
2012, nails, thread on wooden
board, realized by Pamela
Campagna

6 NETwork 02
2011, nails, thread on wooden
board, realized by Pamela
Campagna in collaboration with
Thomas Scheiderbauer

Frank Plant

Gavin Worth

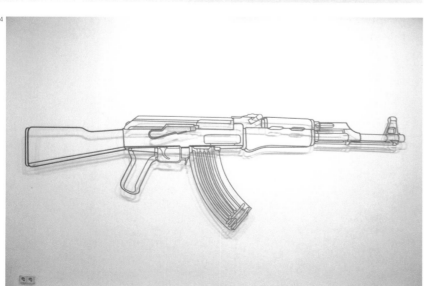

Maurizio Anzeri
1–6 **I Will Be With You On Your Wedding Night.**
2012, embroidery on photo,
Courtesy of the artist, private
collection
1 No. 8
2 No. 5
3 No. 6
4 No. 3
5 No. 1
6 No. 4

Paper-Cut-Project
1 Client: The Bay, 2010, Bristol paper, glue
2–4 **Spring/summer 2012 runway,** Client: Jen Kao, Spring/Summer 2012 runway, Bristol, glue Photos: Paper-Cut-Project

MIRROR
MIRROR

"The self is not given to us, ... there is only one practical consequence: we have to create ourselves as a work of art."

Michel Focault

Akatre
1   Festivals été
    Client: Libération, 2011
2–3 Retromania
    Client: Libération, 2012
    vinyl discs

Robert G. Bartholot
4–5 Mariä
    Client: Œ Magazine, Berlin, 2011
6–7 Client: Première Classe, Paris,
    2011

4

6

5

7

Robert G. Bartholot

1-2 **Classic Nightmares**
2010

3 **I AM**
Client: Manifesto Magazine,
Design Republic, China, 2012

4 **Le Cube**
Client: Who's Next, Paris, 2012

5 **Mister Brown**
Client: Who's Next, Paris, 2012

Robert G. Bartholot
Geometric Homicide
2009

Reddish—Design Studio
Untitled—Profiles Project
2011, aluminum, Photos: Dan
Lev Studio

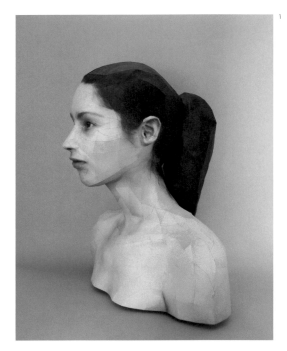

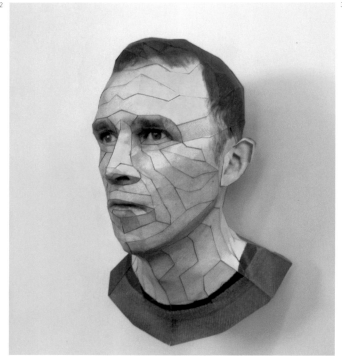

Bert Simons
1 Portrait of Rozemarijn Lucassen
   2008, paper, inkjet print
2 Portrait of Mr. Ivo Opstelten
   2009, paper, inkjet print
3 Self Portrait
   2006, paper, inkjet print

Mathilde Roussel
4 Lives of Grass
   2010, soil, wheat seeds, recycled metal,
   fabric, Photos: Matthieu Raffard
5 Mue
   2011, paper, glue, Photos: Matthieu Raffard

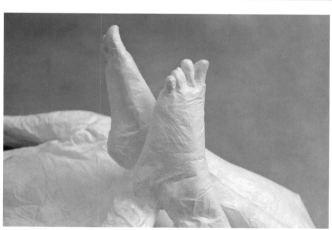

**Emmanuelle Moureaux
Architecture + Design**

1 Toge
   Photos: Daisuke Shimokawa /
   Nacasa & Partners Inc.

Daisy Balloon

2–3 Expressive Balloons
     2009, Photos: Hiroshi Manaka,
     Hair & Make-up: Rie Suda, Post-
     production: Yoshiaki Sakurai

4 The Art of Layering
   2010, Photo: Hiroshi Manaka,
   Head Stylist: Kunio Kohzaki,
   Make-up: Ebara

5 The Moment in a Springs
   Client: Osaka Takashimaya, 2012,
   Photos: Hiroshi Manaka, Post-
   production: Yoshiaki Sakurai,
   Make-up: Ken Nakano, Hair: Koji
   Ichikawa, Stylist: Koji Oyamada,
   Curation: Daisuke Nagamori,
   Naohito Miyagi, Momoko Yamada

next spread Forest Apple Bear
   2011, Photo: Hiroshi Manaka,
   Make-up: Ebara, Hair: Koji Ichikawa, Stylist: Koji Oyamada, Post-
   production: Yoshiaki Sakurai, Set
   Production: Yoshihito Tada

Tomaas
Plastic Fantastic
2010, plastic, Photos: Tomaas,
Stylist: Carla Engler, Make-
up: Fiona Thatcher, Hair: Seiji
Uehara, Post production: Elena
Levenets

Frédérique Daubal
¹ Hide & Seek
2010
² Big Eyes
2012, Photo: Johanna Salomez
³ Big Mouth
2012, Photo: Johanna Salomez

Iris van Daalen
⁴⁻⁶ Graphical Hair
⁴ Crown of Hair
⁵ Shoulder Pads
⁶ Crown of Hair
2010, hair, resin
Concept & Styling: Iris van
Daalen, Photos: Lisa Klappe

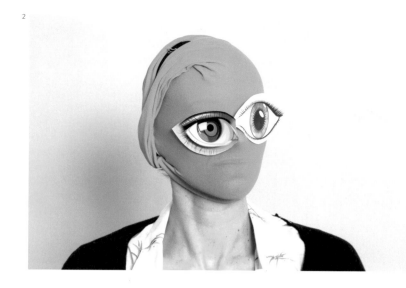

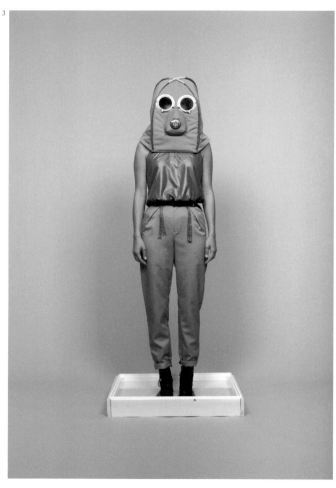

Femke Agema
1 Nigliktok—Frost Suit
2 Drijf—Pants Outfit
3 Drijf—Mask Outfit
4 Nigliktok—Snowflake Suit
   Outfit from Autumn/Winter
   2012/2013 collection,
   Photos: Roel Determeijer

Robert Hardgrave
5 Rapture Suit
   2010, acrylic, canvas, thread,
   Photo: Christopher Nelson

Tom Darracott
6–8 Fabric
   Client: Fabric nightclub,
   London, 2008, cardboard, paint

Alt Group
1 Silo Theatre
   Photo: Toaki Okano, Agency: Alt
   Group, Creative Director: Dean
   Poole, Design Team: Dean Poole,
   Anna Myers, Aaron Edwards

Corriette Schoenaerts
2 Pillows
3 Sleeping Couple
4 LE—3 Men
5 Newspaper
6 Watering Plants
   Client: LE Carpets, 2010
   Photos: Corriette Schoenaerts,
   In collaboration with Emmeline
   de Mooij

Jessica Walsh
1–5 Client: Aizone, 2011, paint, model, Photos: Henry Hargreaves, Creative Direction: Stefan Sagmeister, Direction & Art Design: Jessica Walsh, Body Painting: Anastasia Durasova

141

Jessica Walsh
 Forget Regret
 Client: Aizone, 2011, paint,
 model, Photo: Henry Harg-
 reaves, Creative Direction: Ste-
 fan Sagmeister, Direction & Art
 Design: Jessica Walsh, Body
 Painting: Anastasia Durasova

INSENSIBLE

LES VEGETAUX SONT DES ETRES VIVANTS NON DOUES, COMME LES ANIMAUX, DE SENSIBILITE ET DE MOTILITE

INEBRANLABLE

FIXE

FIGE

IMPERTURBABLE

INDIFFERENT

ORDNUNG!

_____

"There is no chance
and anarchy in the
universe. All is system
and gradation.
Every god is there sitting
in his sphere."

Ralph Waldo Emerson

Maïssa Toulet
Les Végétaux
2008, bisque doll, plastic and
wood toys, dried vegetals,
plaster, plastic plants, seeds

145

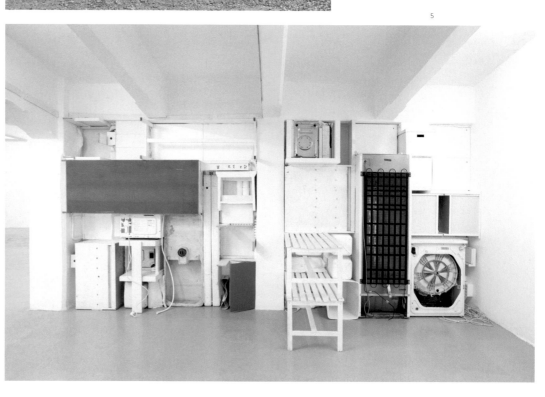

Michael Johansson

¹ **The Move Overseas**
Beaufort04—Triennial of
Contemporary Art by the Sea,
Belgium, 2012, containers,
household items

² **Half Full**
2011, glass table, glass objects

³ **Mind the Gap**
Sølyst Castle Park, Jyderup,
Denmark, 2010, cool boxes,
sun chairs, picnic tables, swing,
garden equipment

⁴ **Domestic Kitchen Planning**
2010, kitchen stool, kitchen
equipment

5 & next spread   **Ghost V**
The Flat—Massimo Carasi, Mi-
lan, Italy, 2011, white furniture,
white objects

Brittany Powell

1 **Mondrian Sandwich**
   2012, dark rye bread, goat's milk gouda, Tillamook cheddar, tomato, lettuce

2 **Johns Sandwich**
   2012, white bread, salami, prosciutto, Tillamook cheddar

3 **Christo and Jeanne-Claude Sandwich**
   2012, Dave's Killer Bread, New York cheddar, salami, tomato, lettuce, dill mustard

4 **Hirst Sandwich**
   2012, white bread, Tillamook cheddar, lettuce, ketchup, yellow mustard, spicy brown mustard

5 **O'Keeffe Sandwich**
   2012, white bread, goat's milk gouda, Tillamook cheddar, lettuce, ketchup, mayonnaise

6 **Pollock Sandwich**
   2012, Dave's Killer Bread, New York cheddar, yellow mustard, ketchup

7 **Rothko Sandwich**
   2012, white bread, Tillamook cheddar, smoked gouda, yellow mustard
   Photos: Brittany Powell

150

Carl Kleiner

1. **5000 SEK**
   Client: Ikea, 2011, carpet, cutlery, china, napkins, flowers
2. **7000 SEK**
   Client: Ikea, 2011, chairs, table, cutlery, china, napkins
3. **Mandelmussla**
   Client: Ikea, 2010, sugar, butter, cloudberries, cream, almonds, flour, egg, currants
4. **Drömmar**
   Client: Ikea, 2010, flour, butter, baking powder, water, sugar
5. **Vaniljhorn**
   Client: Ikea, 2010, butter, flour, vanilla pods, vanilla seeds, sprinkles
   Styling: Evelina Kleiner

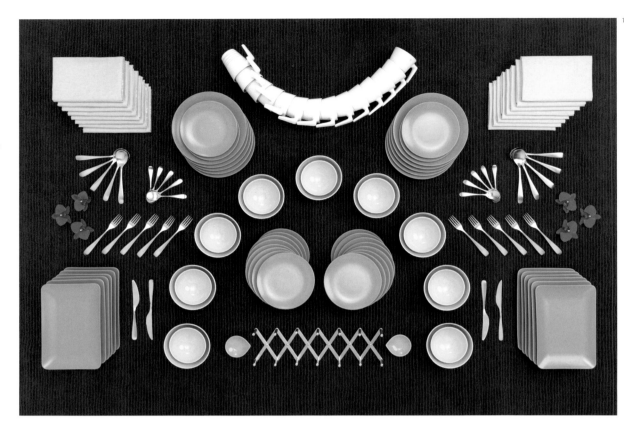

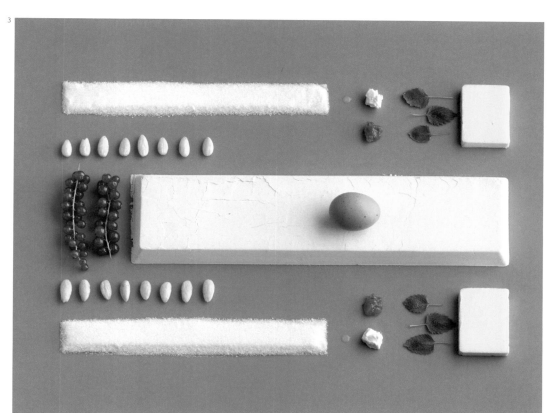

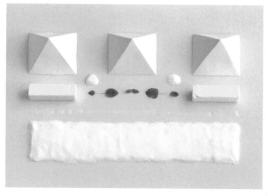

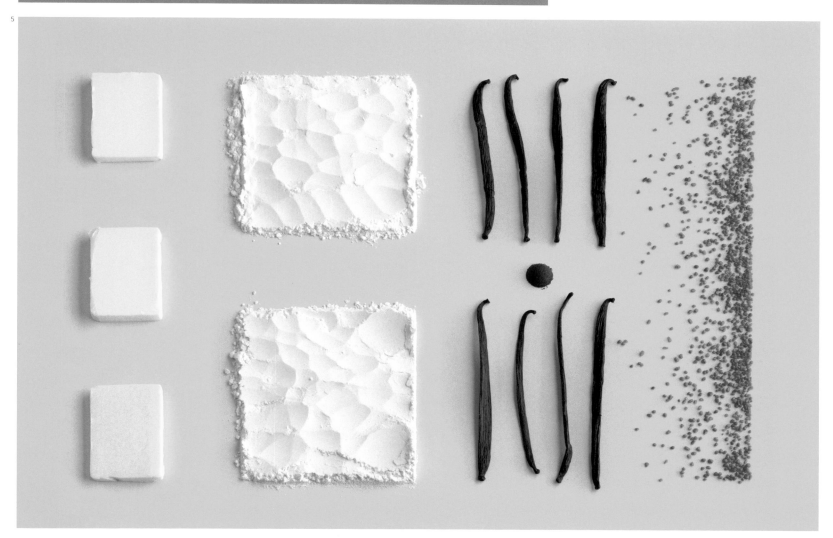

153

Carl Kleiner

[1] **Sportigare jul**
Client: Intersport, 2011, shoes, boxing gloves, shuttle cocks, skateboard wheels, skateboard, baseballs, darts, table tennis racket, Styling: Evelina Kleiner

Kyle Bean

[2] **Aerotropolis**
Client: Financial Times Magazine, 2011, wood, pins, paper, die-cast mini planes, Photo: Beate Sonnenberg

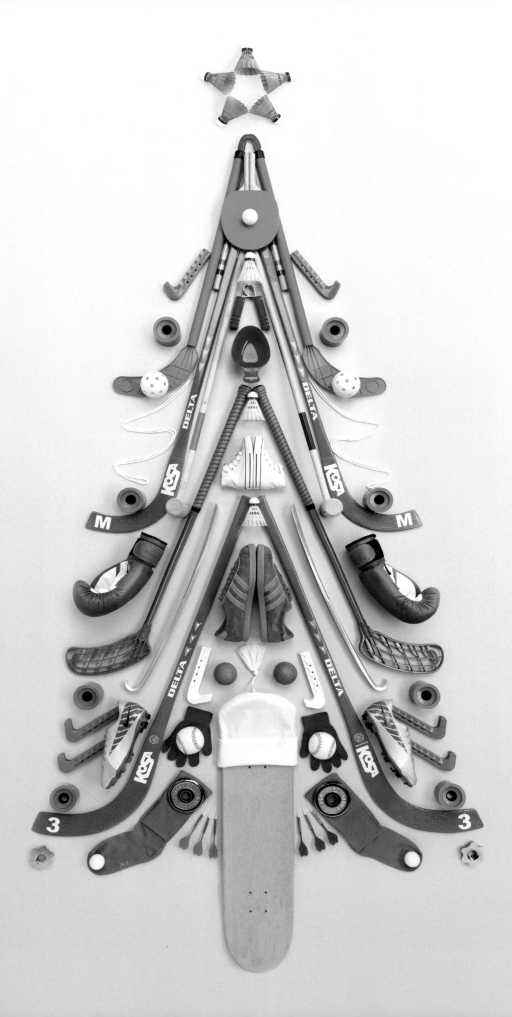

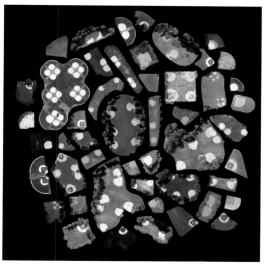

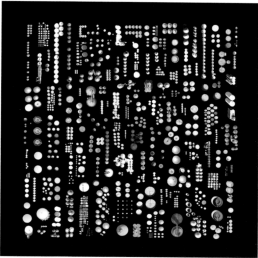

Jenny Odell
1   195 Yachts, Barges, Cargo Lines, Tankers, and Other Ships
2   Every Baseball Diamond in Manhattan
3   1,376 Grain Silos, Water Towers & Other Cylindrical Industrial Buildings
4   104 Airplanes
2009–2011, archival digital print

Krüger & Pardeller
Untitled, MAK 01
Museum of Applied Arts |
Contemporary Art, Vienna,
2012, wood, acrylic,
aluminum, LED lights,
Photo: MAK, Georg Mayer

Rachel Thorlby
1   Long Lost in the Forgetfulness
    of the Forgotten VIII
    2010
2   Long Lost in the Forgetfulness
    of the Forgotten VII
    2010
3   Long Lost in the Forgetfulness
    of the Forgotten I
    2010

DIRECTOR'S CUT

———

"Every act of creation is first of all an act of destruction."

Pablo Picasso

Lucas Simões
1 Unmemory M.R.H.
   2011, 10 cut-out photographs
   and acrylic boards
2 Unportrait—mora na filosofia
   2011, 10 cut-out photographs
   and acrylic boards
3 Unmemory C.M.
   2011, 10 cut-out photographs
   and acrylic boards
4 Unmemory M.E.
   2011, 10 cut-out photographs
   and acrylic boards

Kasia Korzeniecka & Szymon Roginski

[1] Piramid
Client: Anna Kuczynska, 2008
paper, glue, Photo: Katarzyna
Korzeniecka / Szymon Roginski

[2] K-dron
Client: Anna Kuczynska, 2008
paper, glue, Photo: Katarzyna
Korzeniecka / Szymon Roginski

[3] Fair Trade 1
Client: Kikimora Magazine /
Fair Trade, 2010, mosaic made
of clothes

[4] Fair Trade 2
Client: Kikimora Magazine / Fair
Trade, 2010, mosaic made from
different types of coal and
textile bags

2

Kent Rogowski
1–3 Love = Love
1 #1
2006
2 #9
2008
3 #8
2008
store-bought jigsaw puzzles

3

Lauren Hillebrandt
1 Flat Landscapes 01
   2011, paper, plastic cup, C-print
2 Flat Landscapes 02
   2011, paper, nature, C-print

Carl Kleiner
3 Icosahedron 1
   2011, paper, glue
4 Golden Triangle 1
   2011, paper, glue

Kulte
5 Colorama
   Spring/Summer 2012 collection, Kulte fabrics, Photos:
   Mothi Limbu

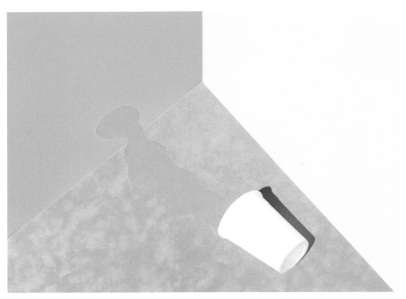

168

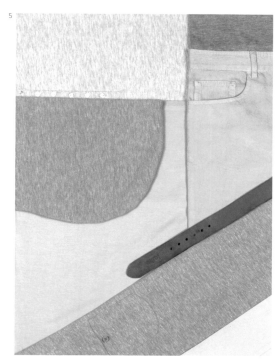
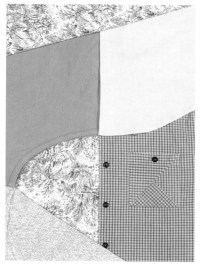
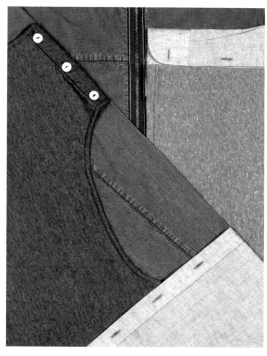
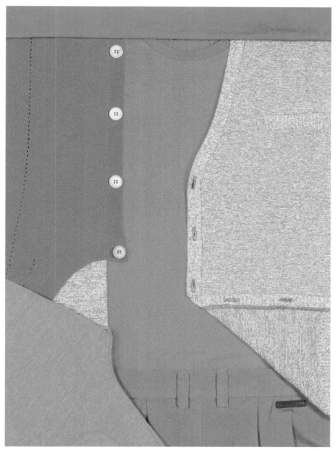

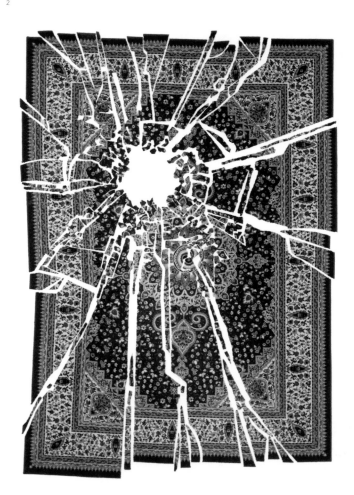

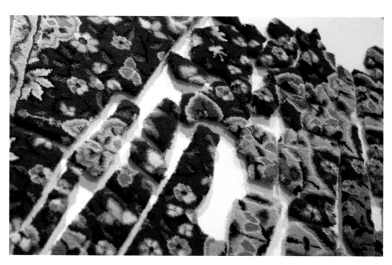

Richard Hutten
1 Playing with Tradition
Client: I + I Italy, 2008, hand-knotted wool, Photo: I + I Italy

Pravdoliub Ivanov
2 Ornaments of Endurance
2011, cut carpet mounted on wall, Courtesy of Krinzinger Gallery, Vienna and Vehbi Koç Foundation, Istanbul
3 Confusion
2002, carpet, baseboard, site-specific work, Courtesy of Collection EPO—Munich

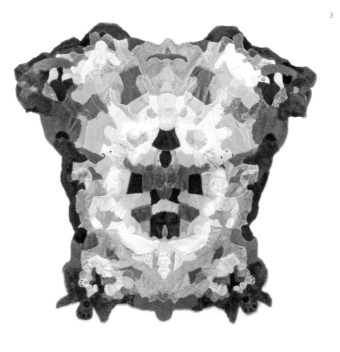

Agustina Woodgate
1   No Rain No Rainbows
2   Royal
3   Home
    2010–2011, stuffed animal skins
    Photos: Spinello Projects

WE MAKE CARPETS
4   Pasta Carpet 2
    2010, dried pasta
5   Army Carpet
    2010, plastic toy soldiers
6   Fork Carpet
    2010, plastic forks

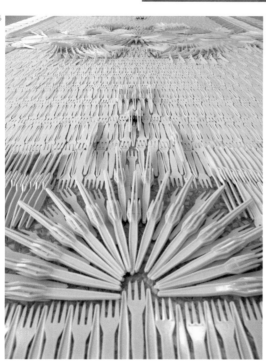

173

SPACE INVADERS

"Thus the wise man looks into space, ... for he knows that there is no limit to dimension."

Lao Tzu

Penique Productions
El claustro
Client: CutOut Fest 2011,
plastic, parcel tape, fans,
Photo: Penique Productions

Penique Productions

1. **Bathroom**
   2008
2. **El Sótano de La Tabacalera**
   Client: CSA La Tabacalera, 2011
3. **Palazzo Ducale**
   Sala Dogana Hands-On Transformation, 2011
4. **Sala Buit**
   2011
5. **Choko Ho'ol**
   2011, plastic, parcel tape, fan
   Photos: Penique Productions

Daniele Papuli
1–2 **Cartoframma**
Castello Aragonese, Otranto, Italy, 2011, "paper diaphragm" made from 10,380 strips of white glossy paper, Photos: Salvatore Basile
3 **Panta Rei**
Villa Soranzo, Varallo Pombia, Italy, 2005 / 2010, lamellar structures made of cardboard strips of various types, installation with 12 pieces in 4 colors, Photo: Enzo Pellitteri

Jenene Nagy
4–5 **out / look**
Washington State University Art Gallery, 2010, Tyvek, latex, Photos: Reza Safavi

179

Henrique Oliveira

1 **Desnatureza**
Galerie Vallois, Paris, 2011, ply-wood, Photo: Aurélien Mole

2 & next spread **Bololô**
Smithsonian National Museum of African Art, Washington, D.C., 2011, plywood

3 **The Origin of the Third World (external view)**
29th São Paulo Biennial, 2010, plywood, PVC, metal

4 **Tapumes**
Rice Gallery, Houston, 2009, plywood, Photo: Nash Baker

181

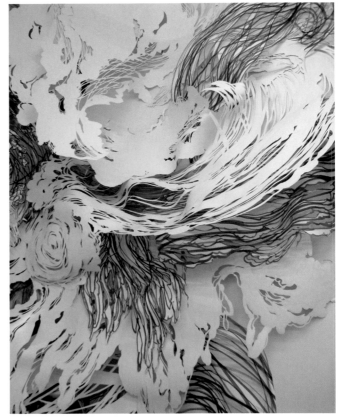

Mia Pearlman
1–2 Penumbra
2010, paper, India ink, paper-clips, tacks

Andreas Kocks
3 Paperwork #505
Leopold-Hoesch-Museum,
2005, watercolor paper,
Photo: Anne Gold
4 Paperwork #502T
2005, tarpaper, Photo: Hermann
Feldhaus

Andreas Kocks
1   Paperwork #936(3)G, "Splatter II"
     Neue Galerie Dachau, 2009,
     graphite on watercolor paper,
     Photo: Jan Schünke, Courtesy of
     Sebastian Fath Contemporary
2   Paperwork #701G,
     "In the Beginning"
     DG Galerie, Munich, 2007,
     graphite on watercolor paper,
     Photo: Christoph Knoch

Gabriel Dawe

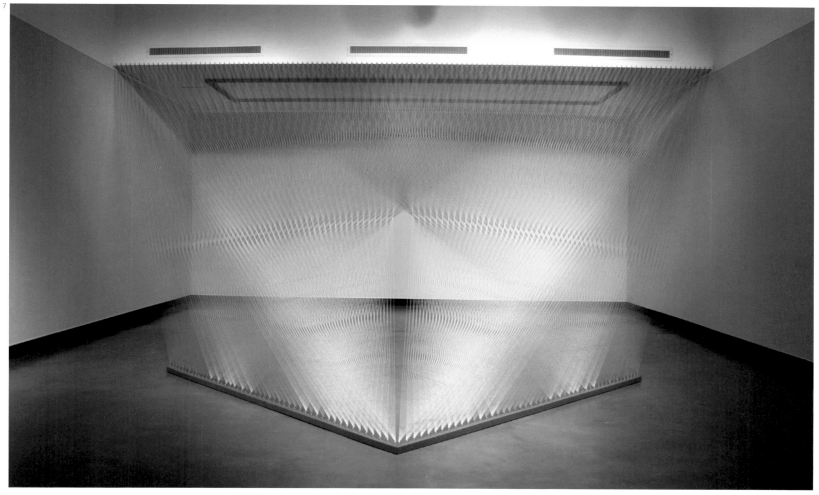

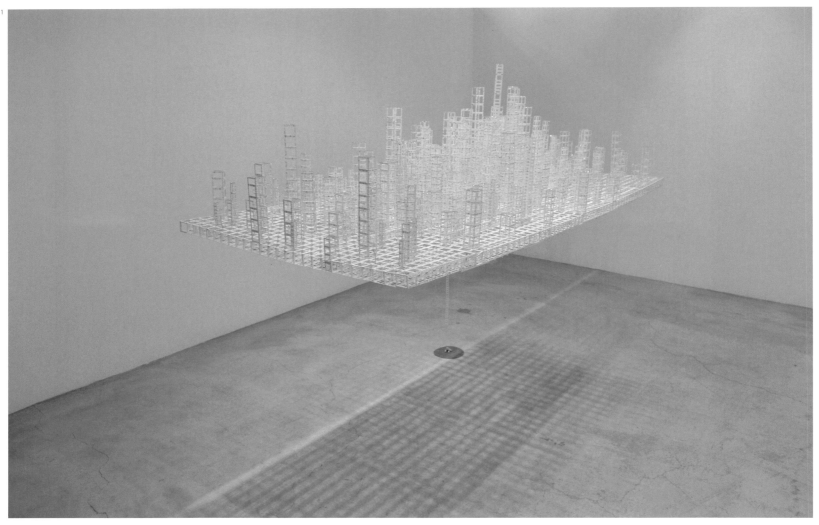

Katsumi Hayakawa
1   Floating City
    2011, paper, glue, inkjet prints,
    glitter, wire
2   Detail of Composition 16
    2011, paper, glue, gouache,
    inkjet prints, etc. on paper
3   Detail of Level 30
    2011, paper, glue, gouache,
    inkjet prints, etc. on paper

Alida Rosie Sayer
4   A Vanishing Point
    2011, hand-painted acetate
    sheets, scaffolding frame,
    Photos: Philip Sayer

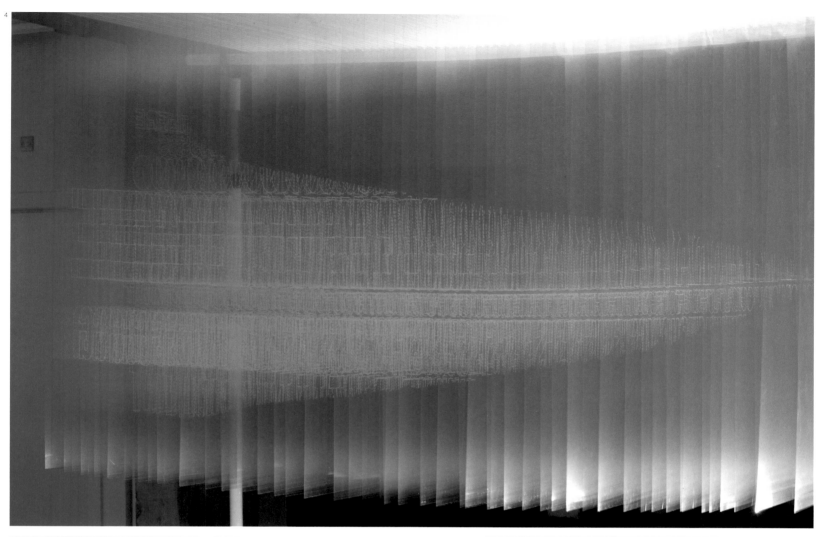

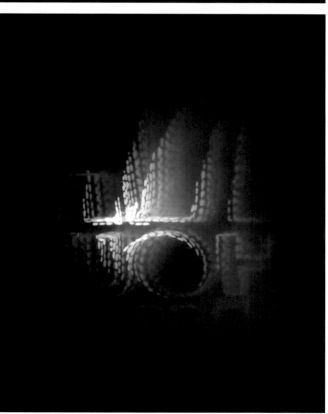

Charles Clary
1–2 Flameobic Opulation
2010, acrylic, hand-cut paper on panel
3 Double Diddle Evisceration (Detail)
2009, acrylic, hand-cut paper on panel
Photos: Charles Clary

Michael Kukla
4 Stratal 312
2012, laminated plywood
5 Kuro #1
2010, black slate
6 Stratal 310
2010, laminated plywood

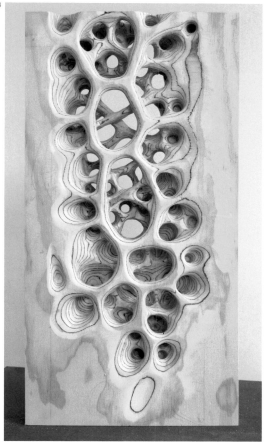

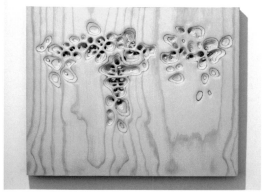

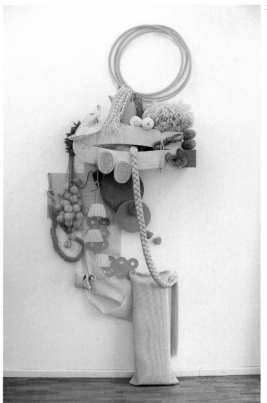

Denise Julia Reytan
1–2 **Consumwave**
2008, all you can find in a de-
partment store, in collaboration
with Bjoern Wolf
3 **Big Poem**
2010
Photos: D.J.R.

VARIETY OF THE SPECTACLE

"Every action, every artwork, ... every physical scene, drawings on the blackboard, performance, brings a new element in the whole, an unknown area, an unknown world."

Joseph Beuys

Malene Hartmann Rasmussen
1   If I Had A Heart I Could Love You
    2011, ceramics, MDF, polyester
    fiber, pins, embroidery,
    digital print, found object,
    Photos: Ester Segarra

Megan Whitmarsh
2   Color Work Station
    2009, fabric, embroidery
    thread, polyfill, luan, paint,
    marker, wire, vinyl,
    Courtesy of Michael
    Rosenthal Gallery

Judy Kameon | Elysian Landscapes
1   Plants x T
    Client: The New York Times
    Style Magazine, 2011,
    130 plants, in collaboration with
    Erik Otsea, Photo: Erik Otsea,

Karim Charlebois-Zariffa
2   The New York Times
    Magazine cover
    2011, balloons, string, tape,
    Photo: Tom Schierlitz,
    Assistants: Benjamin Bryant,
    Paul Fuog

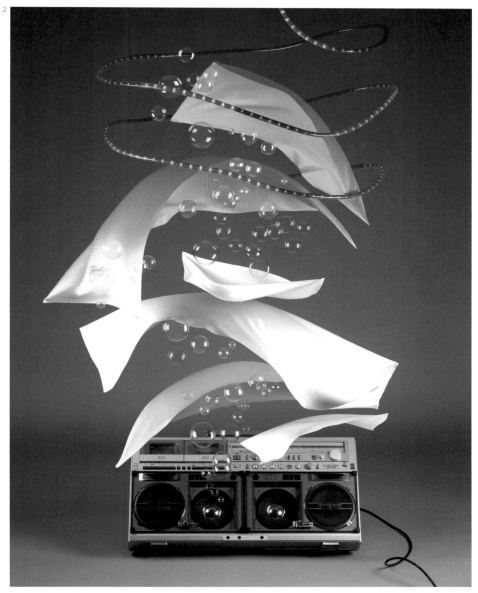

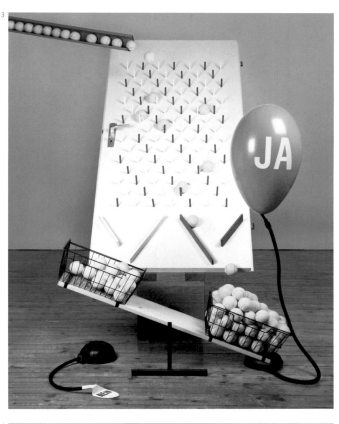

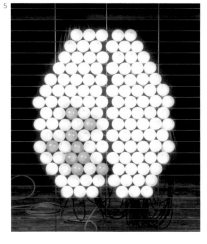

Katrin Schacke

1 **The Development of Thoughts and Memories**
Client: Süddeutsche Zeitung Magazin, 2011,
600 table tennis balls, 21 filling funnels,
3 white containers, 1 plastic bowl

2 **The Great Illusion of Free Will**
Client: Süddeutsche Zeitung Magazin, 2011,
1 door, tennis balls, 2 baskets, air pumps,
ballons, rain pipe

3 **The Correlation of Music and Intelligence**
Client: Süddeutsche Zeitung Magazin, 2011,
ghetto blaster, scarves, soap bubbles, wind,
illuminated flexible tube

4 **Labyrinth**
Client: sushi 13 (yearbook of the Art Directors Club Germany), 2011, big electric bulb,
black cable, wood

5 **The Art of Reading Human Minds**
Client: Süddeutsche Zeitung Magazin, 2011,
white and orange electric bulbs, black and
orange cables

Matthew Plummer-Fernandez
1   Apifera
    Client: Selfridges, 2008,
    card, computer fans, Arduino,
    electronics

Foam
2   Dry the River Horses
    (a 3D papercraft poster project)
    Client: RCA Label Group (UK),
    2011, Creative Directors: Phil
    Clandillon & Steve Milbourne,
    Creative: Xavier Barrade,
    Producer: Simon Poon Tip,
    Director: Ricky Stanton, Photo:
    Xavier Barrade

Don Lucho / Luis Valdés
3   Economía de Recursos
    2009

204

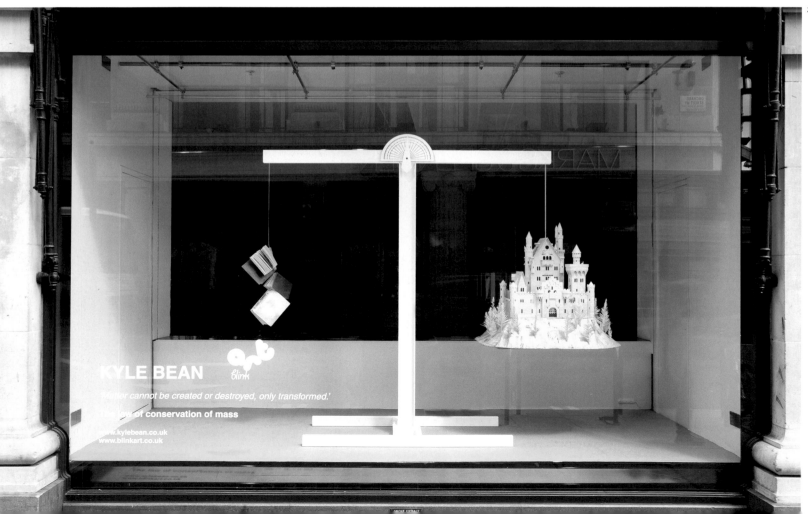

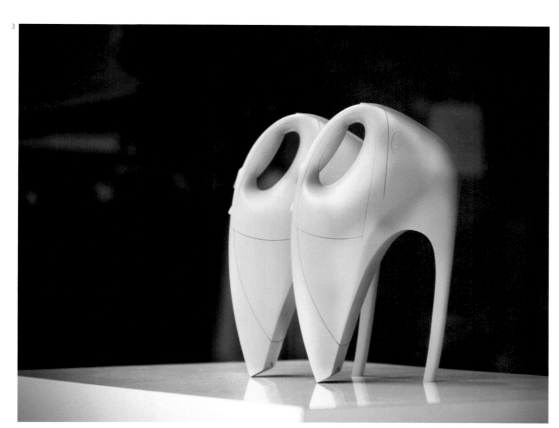

Kyle Bean
1 **Transformation—Box**
cardboard, string, metal frame
2 **Transformation—Books**
Client: Selfridges, 2010,
fairytale books, paper,
metal frame
Photos: Mike Dodd

Lernert & Sander
3 **Selfridges**
Client: Selfridges, 2010,
Production: Blinkart,
Photos: Lex Kembery

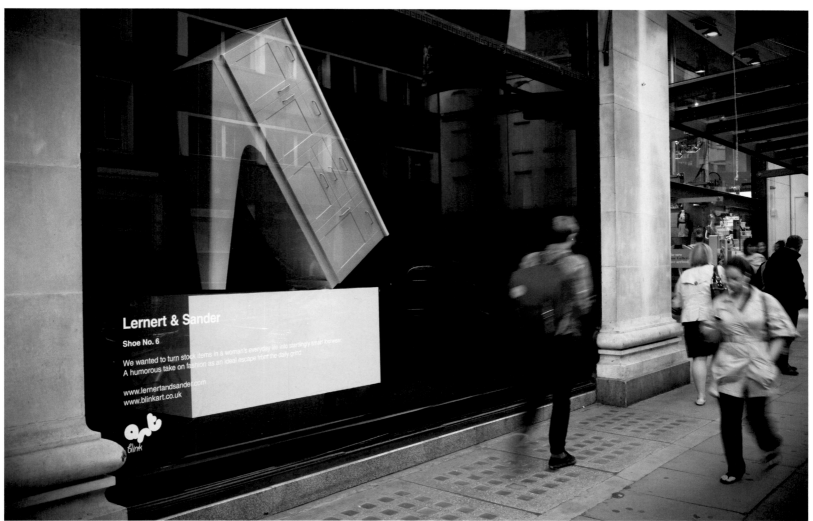

Lernert & Sander

Shoe No. 6

We wanted to turn stock items in a woman's everyday life into startlingly smart footwear.
A humorous take on fashion as an ideal escape from the daily grind.

www.lernertandsander.com
www.blinkart.co.uk

Kyle Bean
Transformation—Motorbike
Client: Selfridges, 2010,
2 identical motorbikes, steel
frame fabrication, metal wire,
Photo: Andrew Meredith

Byggstudio
Folkets Park Entrance—
Sign Concept
Client: Folkets Park, 2010,
Photo: Lotten Pålsson

The Glue Society
1   It Wasn't Meant to End Like This
2009, earth, excavator
2   I Wish You Hadn't Asked
2011
Photos: Nicolai Lorenzen

Dorota Buczkowska
1 Swing
   2008, latex, Styrofoam, helium,
2 Infection
   2008, plastic, helium
3 Black Swing
   2008, plastic, Styrofoam, helium

Willy Chyr
4&6 Ondine
   2011, balloons, fishing wires,
   video projector
5 Roller Coaster
   2011, balloons, fishing wires
7 Balluminescence
   Client: Science Chicago, 2009,
   balloons, PVC pipes, fishing
   wire, wood, Photo: Jasmine
   Kwong
8-9 Eye Candy
   Client: gh3 Architects and
   Landscape Architects, 2011,
   balloons, fishing wire,
   Photo: Joel Di Giacomo

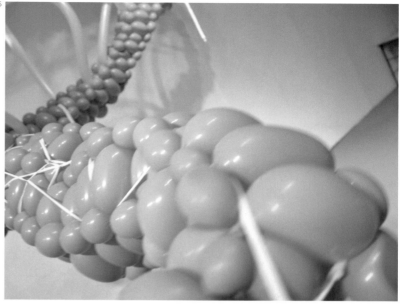

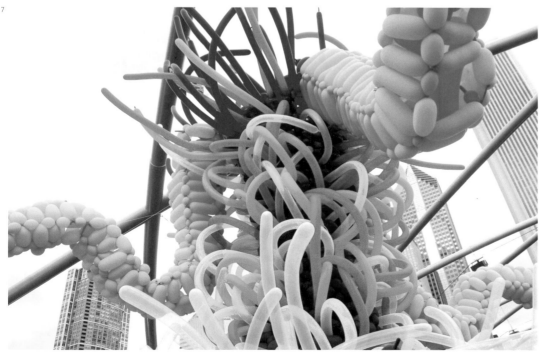

Filippo Minelli
1 Shape No. 5
2 Shape No. 9
3 Shape No. 19
4 Shape No. 10
2012–2012, pigments,
chemicals, landscape

Ujin Lee
5–8 Dust Series—Bypass
5 Bypass
6 Printers
7 Park
next spread Playground
2009
Photos: Ujin Lee & Tom Edwards

ADDRESS
INDEX
